JackJack & JuneBug

A Love Song in Poems and Posts

Marilyn June Coffey and Jack Loscutoff

OMEGA
COTTONWOOD
PRESS

Omaha, Nebraska

JACKJACK & JUNEBUG: A LOVE SONG IN POEMS AND POSTS

Paperback ISBN-13: 978-0-9961399-4-6
Library of Congress Control Number: 2015960973
Cataloging in Publication Data on file with publisher.

Omega Cottonwood Press
13518 L St.
Omaha, NE 68137

PRODUCTION, DISTRIBUTION AND MARKETING:
Concierge Marketing Inc. www.ConciergeMarketing.com

PHOTO CREDITS:
Jack and Marilyn, pg. x – David Loyd
Jack Loscutoff, pg. 37 – Portraits Now
Marilyn June Coffey, David Loyd and Lobsang Wangchuk, pg. 44 – Deirdre Evans
Marilyn June Coffey, pg. 51 – David Loyd

Printed in the United States
10 9 8 7 6 5 4 3 2 1

Praise for JackJack & JuneBug

"Jack was one of my favorite people, period. I loved the way his mind worked, I savored his colorful comments. He was brilliant."

—Dan Reynolds, fellow author

"May you have many more charming happenings. Of course I am also selfish. I like reading about them."

—Wayne Anson, Nebraska Writers Guild President

"You are quite marvelous to not spare yourself with your grief and then to be brave enough not to hide it from others!"

—Barbara Schmitz, winner of 2015 NE Center for the Book

"Glad for the teeny eensie pill."

—Marilyn Ray, MD

"Wonderful, Marilyn. Just perfect."

—Beverly Walker, Editor, Rockstone Press

"You take your love story all the way to Heaven!"

—Bob Schmitz

"I'm happy to read your missives. They're so human, so clear."

—Linda Trichter Metcalf, Ph.D., Director, Proprioceptive Writing Center

"A heartwarming story."

—George Lauby, Editor, The North Platte Bulletin newspaper.

"The things that you have been writing have been very touching."

—Greg Kosmicki, Poet, Editor Emeritus of The Backwaters Press

"You are so quirky! And another thing I love about you is your honesty."

—Carole Rosenthal, Prof. Emeritus, Pratt Institute.

For Bee and Sandy, my cheerleaders

JackJack & JuneBug

Contents

Part III: Mourning Jack

Biographies of

Marilyn June Coffey & Jack Loscutoff

When Marilyn and Jack met in 2008, both were proficient lovers. Each had weathered two marriages that ended in divorce and one long-term relationship that ended in death. Plus who knew how many short-term lovers. Dozens, certainly.

Marilyn and Jack wasted little time living in the past, enthusiastically creating a new present. Once a day, minimum. Usually twice. And three or more times on those days when they couldn't keep their hands off each other.

Jack exhibited a strong artistic bent. He chronicled their physical relationship through photos. He snapped many color pictures of Marilyn in the nude, and some of himself. Well, not altogether naked. He liked photos of Marilyn in nothing but her red hat. One winter, he coaxed her into a snowy outdoors wearing only boots and mittens and wielding a snow shovel. "June in January," he called that series.

Their relationship, often idyllic, could also be rocky. One day Marilyn threw Jack out of their home, and he went to live with his son's family. But once she had gotten his attention, they negotiated a return that lasted until he left for assisted living in 2015.

Jack and Marilyn weren't young. He was seventy-seven when they met; she seventy-one. In the nearly seven years they spent together, they watched each other age. They witnessed their former three-times-a-day become a memory, then twice, and after monumental resistance, then once.

By that time, their passion had matured into tenderness, adoration, and compassion. Still, right to the end, they couldn't keep their hands off each other.

INTRODUCTION

Thursday, December 4, 2008, 1:13 p.m.

TO MARILYN FROM BILLIE WALKER

WHAT??????????????? You have a beau and didn't tell me! You hussy! Please, I have to know all the details. Where did you meet him???? How long has this been going on? Oh, Marilyn, I am so happy for you.

Thursday, December 4, 2008, 4:48 p.m.
To Billie from Marilyn

His name is Jack Loscutoff, he's a young seventy-seven, and we met in our writing group. He wooed me by being interested in my writing (he writes poetry, sci-fi novels, and plays). Promised to be my coach.

We met off and on. Jack was a real gentleman, a little peck on the cheek goodbye, and meantime, I had the hots for him. But after our slow start, things moved Very Quickly. Didn't take me too long to figure out that Jack is the most sophisticated lover I'd ever had. He lives north of me about 6 miles in his own house. We sleep together every night, his place or mine, whichever's handy, spend all day Sunday with each other. That's guaranteed minimum. We also hang out together a lot in between those times.

We're a good match, and each of us deliriously happy to have found the other. I never expected to make it to Heaven, but it seems as though I'm getting at least an Advance Preview.

Can I tell the Red Hat girls about your new beau?

Of course. Did I mention he is handsome, likes to tell the kind of bad jokes that make you groan, and thinks I'm the best thing since homemade mashed potatoes?

3

Part I: Courtship

The Mentor

I met Jack Loscutoff when I joined the Omaha Nightwriters' Fiction Collective, about eight or ten writers who met monthly in the basement of the old Bookworm bookstore to critique each other's work.

Jack always attended. A big sort of bushy man, he had a lion's head of hair. But he looked old, gray, rather stooped.

He seemed macho to me, talking too long and too loudly, halfway deaf, I found out later. Conceited, he always had something to say. He liked to make detailed comments about this and that, not always directly related to the topic at hand. A motor mouth, sometimes laced with such colorful language or sarcasm that our leader struggled to constrain Jack.

However, he, sharp as a whip and funny, had a positive side. He seemed born to criticize writing. He'd studied halfway to a PhD in English and American literature, and he'd analyzed the best: Fyodor Dostoevsky, Leo Tolstoy, Henry James, Herman Melville, Mark Twain. Critiquing us mere mortals? A piece of cake for Jack.

Then, a surprise. I received an email from him asking me if I had rewritten my Dorothy Parker piece, the manuscript our group had just reviewed.

Parker, a witty writer of the 1920s, used sarcasm that exceeded even Jack's. Stan Isler, my previous lover, had died in 2004 on the Fourth of July, ruining a perfectly good holiday for me. However, he had given me Dorothy Parker's writing case, which he had acquired in a highly roundabout way when his brother, a collector, died. I struggled to write Stan's story.

I sent my revised copy to Jack, and he invited me to discuss it over coffee at Border's, a big bookstore that hadn't yet collapsed. Always eager for feedback on my writing, I accepted.

I stood buying my coffee at the counter when Jack showed up. He stopped a ways away, looking for me. A wonder in beige. I scanned down his tan face across his khaki trench coat to the crotch of his rumpled café au lait pants. My groin rumbled. "Marilyn," I thought. "Have you no shame?" But the spasm was unmistakable.

We sat at a tiny table, hemmed and hawed.

"Your Parker piece interests me," he glanced at me, his face soft. "I'd like to be your mentor—"

Jack, an experienced guide! Great!

Until he said, "If you promise to do everything I tell you to."

I whooped. My laughter ricocheted off the ceiling of the coffee shop.

Jack kept right on talking, about Scrabble, I think.

Later, he repeated his offer but without his ludicrous addendum.

I accepted. I had to honor my groin, still twitching.

—Marilyn June Coffey

Centaur

This horse I ride is slowing down,
forgets the way to barn from town;
once could gallop, now just trots
lame and winded; needs more shots,

needs more potions, needs more pills
to treat his geriatric ills;
always grazing, chewing hay,
awake by night, a-snore by day;

long of tooth but short of sense,
tries to jump, flattens fence;
don't feel his oats, ain't worth his fodder,
can't pull his weight, can't hold his water;

no more fire in the blood,
too fat and tired even for stud.
So why not turn him into
dog food, bone meal, leather, glue?

I've thought of it, but—on the level?
I'm too attached to the old devil.

—Jack Loscutoff

Embodied

I wear my body like a garden glove
whose shape grows less finite
each passing spring

At this rate I'll soon
be forced to discard it
That much seems certain

Too painful the thought!
Why I remember this glove
when it clung to my spirit like kid
stretching and swelling to match
the least wish of each flexing knuckle
I thought I would never reject it
But now to be perfectly blunt
this glove has stretched
its once-tailored self extinct:
fingers hang wrinkled
split seams don't mend
Even its lining has thinned

Inside, my spirit, recalling
kid's snug embrace, drifts
bewildered, an angel fetus
afloat in an elephant's womb

This rag! I should trash it
plow it under for compost—
why delay what time will bring?

But I procrastinate

Like the scent of a departed lover
faded but sweet
this glove clings

—Marilyn June Coffey

October 16, 2008

After Jack and I had seen each other off and on during the autumn of 2008 and shared our poems, I invited him to join me at my favorite coffee shop, Caffeine Dreams.

Typically, I arrived first, bought some coffee (I still drank it then), and sat and waited. Waited and waited and waited until I figured Jack had stood me up.

My abdomen grumbled. I wanted to visit the restroom, but I hesitated. What if Jack showed up and didn't see me?

When the rumble insisted, I dashed to the ladies room, plopped on the toilet at the last minute. Thunder, boom, roar, flush. I leaped away from the toilet in the nick of time to avoid an avalanche, and I fled the room, a flood creeping across the floor behind me.

There Jack sat at a tiny table, coffee in hand.
"Hi!" I cried as I dashed past him to get help.

Later, at the tiny table, we both confessed.
I kept mine as succinct as possible. To my
relief, Jack didn't flinch. Then he elaborated
his confession, explaining street by street how he
thought he'd known Caffeine Dreams's location, but as it turned out, he hadn't.

Later, we walked on Omaha's Field Club trail.

I knew Jack liked me, but he had been a real gentleman, a little peck on the cheek goodbye and that was it. On the trail, we walked carefully side by side, neither touching.

Such good manners grated me, so when we returned to our cars, I turned to Jack and asked, "Are you a hugger?"

Was he! A big bear hug and a kiss on the lips that he swore was my doing and I swore was his.

That was October 16, as close to an anniversary as we ever calculated.

—Marilyn June Coffey

Part II: Passion

My Lion-Headed Lover

never stops wooing me

He rises from eager ardor

to relish the beauty of my spine's arc

with a blunt straight-nailed finger

that signals his constant rapture

His potent arms hourly encircle me

"hello" "goodbye" "whatcha doing?"

as he pulls me into his powerful embrace

Almost as often as breathing

he declares his devotion

in multi-syllabic Latin-based words

cascading from his wine-red lips

as he celebrates cerebration

parses his passion for me

his English intimate in my ear

Even at night, asleep, my lover's

body reaches, stretches, turns

toward me. Magnetized

by thinly veiled veneration,

his warmth constantly seeks mine

as incapable of separating

as the sea is powerless

to ignore a rising moon

—Marilyn June Coffey

MY ONE-EYED LOVER

seldom sleeps
preferring to race the moon's
arc over our erotic ocean.

At night he pulses inside me
weaves wide-awake-dreams
until the sun perforates the sky

Night after day he smiles,
winks, dives, disgorges
his damp love
in my throbbing crevices
smiles, winks, thrums,
dives back in again

Oh how he punctures me
plunges single-handedly
into my deepest orifice
thrusts, twists, probes
awaits the rejoining
twitch that tells him
yes, he is my one my
only one-eyed lover

And when unavoidably
we must wrench apart—

see how he lingers
on my threshold
trading kisses for time

—Marilyn June Coffey

My Greedy Lover

sez he'll let me go
but don't   Instead

he spread my legs
sez he just wants
an itty bitty kiss
then gobbles me
up 'til I'm burning

after that he sez you
can go now but then
he flips me over
bottom-side up
pounces, plunges
thwacks & wallops me
pommels & pulverizes
until I wheeze wind
& he crumples, exhales
an extended groan

I grasp my chance
tip-toe away
but not before I
hear his spent
promise 'Come
back Come back
Just one more kiss'

Not before his hot
  arm encircles my waist
  his moist lips explore
   the nape of my neck

   'Oh, stay a while!'
   he cries, my ravenous
    rapacious voracious
    can't-never-let-me-go
    unquenchable lover

     so again I whisper
     'Yes! O yes-sireejack!'
     as we dulcify, dissolve

—Marilyn June Coffey

Yes! O yes-sireejack!

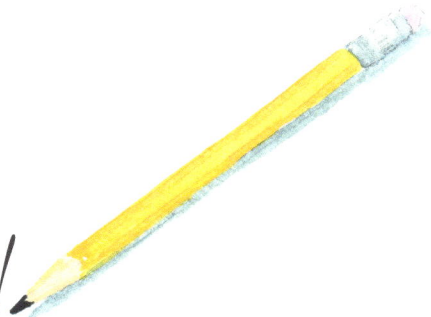

The Gift of Marilyn

She brings me her bright and clever brain
broadcasting from a sculptured,
gray-fringed skull
decorated by little round ears
angled to hear my silly songs of love;
a playful tongue, kissing lips and
truthful eyes within a no-shit Irish
face; soft arms to hold me;
hands to explore me;
a slender, tender vulnerable neck;
her back, a velvet petting plain dropping to
sweet cheeks that part to reveal
a seductive sinkhole; back up to her chest and
full, pink-arrowed breasts;
down to
a whipped cream belly ladled above a split,
hair-whisped hill hiding a
beige flesh flower, her convulsive,
consuming, carnivorous cunt.

—Jack Loscutoff

Daytide, a Friday in February

Your current rushing into my cavity as
predictably as tide swallows the beach

Snow flakes, barely visible, sky-dancing
as I feed five brown squirrels, three black

Scrambling yellow eggs, watching them
metamorphose from liquid into chunks

Watching you read a poetry book,
not me. Feeling your strange silence

Coffee, hot & bitter, on my tongue

Glimmering of blackberry
jam before the knife's slice

Placing a "Forever" stamp on the envelope
holding my HIV report for your former lover

The sting of Mercurochrome
you dab on my cat-claw scratch

Sitting in the car, jazz & heat full blast,
reading about radical feminist dykes,
remembering New York, laughing

Giving you my street address so
the post office will forward your mail

Feeling my masseuse's solid feet on
my spine, her fingers on my face

Picking up a piece of blueberry muffin
I dropped on the brick street. Knowing
better but eating it. Grit in my teeth

Brushing baby snow off the windshield
with the stiff bristly brush you gave me

Hugging, for today's forty-fourth time

The warmth of your naked body on mine
Feeling the tug of your tide. Yielding

—Marilyn June Coffey

My Early Morning Lover

wakes at 2 or 3 or 4

to ask "morning yet?"

Nimble fingers

trace his inquiry

along my spine

beneath my breasts

his breath heavy

in my ear

his silver pistol cocked

awaiting dawn's permit

to navigate my crack

penetrate my cave my hole

"What time is it anyway?"

he pleads, his mouth

full of "honey."

—Marilyn June Coffey

To My Not Quite So New Lover

who no longer drops

after one hundred seven nights

together [minus twice when separate

snow storms kept us apart]

the toilet seat

after he pees

—Marilyn June Coffey

He Leaves

piles of peanut skins beneath his chair
    towels crumpled on the bathroom floor
        a jumble of papers—bills he might pay,
concerts he may attend—on any empty surface
    books by the carload stacked on the floor
        a hodgepodge of laundry moldering in its bin
oodles of might-be-useful plastic bags
    heaps of dirty dishes, collections of paper clips,
        pecks of rubber bands, of bent nails, of screws
a medley of #2 pencils stubs, from short to shorter

    Who is this man?
        My new-found roomy.
            Should I reform him?
                Absolutely not!

I love that he leaves clutter for he also
    leaves tons of immaculate kitty litter
        the right thrust of air pumped in my tires
gobs of hot homemade pancakes on my plate
    & chicken soup & blueberry pie & honey
        reams of delectable love poems, his, to me
drifts of his hot breath caressing my ear
    bunches of kisses nibbled on my neck
        the imprint of his hand daily on my butt
the memories of our nightly pommelings
    accruing in monumental joyful drifts
        left by his burgeoning love for me

                —Marilyn June Coffey

KALEIDOSCOPE

I straddle him
watch his eyelids close
hear him pant.
He doesn't see me bounce
no, it's his first wife
before she hated him
his second wife
before she kicked him out
his third wife, before she died
It's Emily, Anna, Chloe,
Julie, Liz, Sofia
Bev, Kathy, Robin
Lady Chatterley
Molly Bloom
Helen of Troy

I roll over, feel him enter
close my eyes
It's my first husband pounding
before he called me "whore"
my second husband
before he left me
my third husband
before he died
It's Tom, Joe, Aaron,
Dick, Henry, Bill
Chuck, Randy, Gus
Jack Kerouac
Marlon Brando
King Kong

Finished, we rise
blink, startled to see
only each other.

—Marilyn June Coffey

24

A Difficult Spring

April 7, Jack turned 80, which is like turning 50 or 21. A monumental birthday.

Right off, he wrecked his station wagon. A typical 80-year-old crash. Late for an appointment, he drove 35 on a 30 mph stretch with a white car ahead of him. He decided to see how late he was, so he shook his sleeve and consulted his watch. Ten minutes late. He looked up. The white car had stopped dead in the street, and Jack couldn't.

He turned a bit so he smashed the car at an angle, but took out his Volvo's headlight. The other driver, waiting to turn left into her driveway, wasn't hurt. Nor was her car (not much). Nor was Jack. But his ancient red Volvo station wagon sighed and insisted on a ride to Dingman's. When Dingman's offered to fix the car for more $$$ than Jack had paid for it, he bid his baby a reluctant good-bye.

BOOM, we became a one-car family.

To avoid a fine for hitting a car, Jack took a class on safe driving. When the teacher spoke, Jack recognized himself: an occasional runner of red lights, a driver who spaced out and missed Interstate exits, etc. An Unsafe Driver. So he stopped driving.

BOOM, we became a single-driver family. Now I chauffeured Jack everywhere, but especially to doctors' offices across town, where I waited in TV-dominated rooms, struggling to read. Whenever Jack needed groceries or hardware or pills, I sat behind the wheel again.

One doctor convinced Jack that a low-salt diet did not mean eating humongous chunks of cheese. So we got serious, eyeballing sodium in deli cooking, frozen foods, and fast foods. (Oh, we sometimes ate real food. Jack cooked a mean chicken soup, and I learned to stir fry.)

But Jack cried as he ate corn tortillas and no-salt peanut butter. We agreed to eat one solid meal (protein, carb, veggie) a day, so I shopped for it and cooked it. (And ate it: pork chop, corn on the cob, and a yam isn't too bad.) But now I'd become the resident chef. BOOM.

Ten days later, I woke at 5 a.m. feeling uneasy. I ran upstairs to check on Jack. He was in the bathroom.

"How are you?" I hollered through the closed door.

"Sick!"

He'd never admitted sickness. "How sick? Bad sick?"

"No, honey, I'm okay." Jack lurched out of the bathroom and staggered to a chair.

I dialed 911. The ambulance guy said, "Contain your pets," so I herded cats, opened the front door, dressed in street clothes, just in time for the black-rubber-suited boys to put Jack on a stretcher. Hospital doctors diagnosed a urinary infection about to infect Jack's blood stream. Not only that, Jack had worn a pacemaker for a decade. It should have been replaced last year, but it wasn't. The doctors feared that Jack's pacemaker would die—and so would he. But they couldn't replace his pacemaker until his infection cleared up.

After a week, Jack came cheerfully home. Until his surgery healed, he couldn't move his left arm, so BOOM I took over his jobs: hauling out garbage, cleaning litter boxes.

During all this time, I wrote. I snatched an hour here or there to concentrate on a revision of my Dorothy Parker piece. Printed 40 pages to edit in the hospital. Practiced my *Mail-Order Kid* reading.

Friday night, I noticed the toilet running. I called my trusty handyman, "Jack!"

"Oh, I can fix this easy." He put his good arm in the tank, squirreled around, and broke a seal. Now the toilet REALLY ran. "I'll turn the water off," and this he did.

"Turn the water back on any time you need it," he said. Right. If I knew how.

Instead, I hauled out my grandfather's thunder jug for my middle-of-the-night run. Saturday morning, I washed my hair with No Rinse Shampoo, used by NASA's astronauts in space; it made me feel modern.

After that, we discussed marriage.

WHAT? I hear you say. PUT HIM OUT ON THE ICE, the way any sensible Eskimo would do.

But I couldn't.

Where would I find another like Jack, big, bushy and gushing with language? Who would sing 1930s songs and laugh at my stupidest jokes? Who would kiss me at the drop of a hat? Call me his Gracie Allen? Lather me with love?

So we plan to drive to city hall for a license and a judge just as soon as I can mow the lawn, gas the car, take out the garbage, clean the litter boxes, unload the groceries, cook lunch, wash dishes, do the laundry, drive Jack to the hardware store—and finish my Dorothy Parker piece.

—Marilyn June Coffey

MARILYN

(To the Tune of "Rosalie")

Marilyn, my darling, Marilyn, my love,
Every night when push comes to shove,
I know I'm so much in love.
Oh, Marilyn, have mercy.
Do not speak to me of marriage
And a baby carriage,
For I'd decline, Marilyn, mine.
After the cooing and billing,
Please make my life thrilling
And recline, Marilyn mine.

—Jack Loscutoff

MARILYN BE-PISSED ME

Marilyn be-pissed me
   in bed while she sate
      descending onto me;
         marked me as her mate
            as she deigned to screw me.

              With her pee she made her pitch,
                and though I'm still the alpha dog,
                  she's now the top bitch.

                    —Jack Loscutoff

Launch of a Uranus Astronaut

(To the Tune of "Little Brown Jug")

Marilyn and I live all alone
in a house she calls our own.
She loves to suck,
I love to fuck.
Finding each other was great luck.

Ah, ha, ha, you and me.
Generous ass, how I love thee!
Ah, ha, ha, you and me.
Lass with classy ass,
how I love ye!

A rubber band helps Roscoe stand
and do his duty like a man.
Your anus, like a second mouth,
grabs him when'ere he ventures south.

Through its door his head doth poke,
enlarges as he starts to stroke.
Before he can get up to ten,
you convulse with delight and then:

Ah, ha, ha, you and me.
Little pink hole, how we love thee!
Ah, ha, ha, let's fuck some more.
Your tunnel of love, let us explore!

—Jack Loscutoff

30

Vain Anticipation during Elder Copulation

Some day my prick will come.

Some day my dong
will come on real strong.

He'll bing and he'll bang
and he'll bong.
Not quite immaculate,
he will ejaculate.

Some day he will bob, throb and lob
much cum, and you'll say,
"Damned good job!"

—Jack Loscutoff

BELLY RAP

Who knows what lesson a lover may bring.
Take Jack, who caressed my naked stomach and said,
"My, I sure do love your fat little belly."

My fat belly? Surely I misheard. Surely he said, "Flat."

But later, bare-skinned before my mirror,
I had to admit that my flat belly had mysteriously
disappeared.

Like my once brown hair

Like my wisdom teeth

Like my days dissolving into decades.

—Marilyn June Coffey

Our Form of Greeting after Time Apart

For instance:

We slept in separate bedrooms, me in my big basement bedroom and he upstairs in his little room with his $1,000 hospital bed that he could maneuver head or foot.

Jack typically rose earlier than me, so he might be sitting in the dining room, one of his big hands around a cup of coffee, when I skittered upstairs.

Despite two deaf ears, he'd know when I arrived; he'd rise and turn, his arms open. And I'd flee into his embrace.

We specialized in bear hugs, sometimes two or three, with an accompanying fluttering of lips and tongues.

I've read that couples who stay together love the way each partner smelled. And I did love to breathe deep as I wrapped myself around Jack's warm body, his big body when I first knew him, skeletal at the end.

We greeted each other this way each morning and after times when we'd been apart. Increasingly we hugged each other for no particular reason at all. Some days, it felt as though we couldn't get enough of each other.

—Marilyn June Coffey

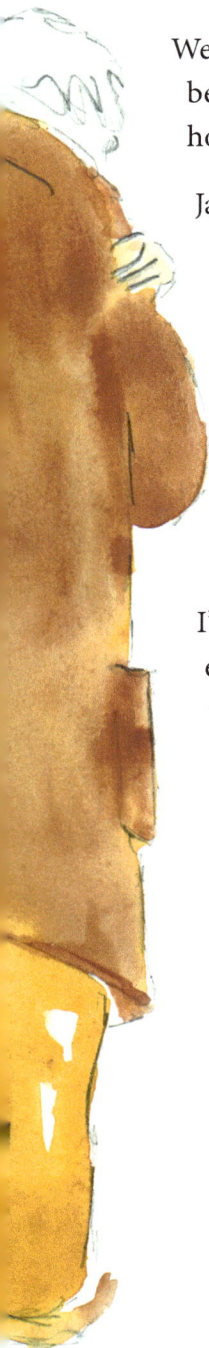

Incredible Closeness

You and Jack had an incredible closeness. Bee

Yes, Bee, we did. The longer we stayed a couple, the deeper it got. The last three months were incredible. We could hardly keep our hands off each other (although he was unable to be a lover by that time, but it didn't matter). And our love for each other became tangible, bonding us whenever we were together. "We're just a couple of teenagers," he'd tell people, his arm around me. I'd never before experienced love of that quality. It bowled me over.

—Barbara "Bee" Lanning and Marilyn June Coffey

Together we sat on a bench outside Crown Pointe

surrounded by evening's warmth

by chattering members of our generation,

and his arm, nonchalant around my shoulders,

misted my eyes.

—Marilyn June Coffey

E-Gads!

Today, September 3, 2015, palliative care called from the hospital and invited me to a little get-together in Jack's room with Jack's son, Mark, and Mark's wife, Jeannette.

Palliative care whisked in wearing a white jacket, obviously in charge.

She enumerated some of Jack's problems: pneumonia, low platelets in his blood, edema, blood that won't coagulate, weight loss, lack of protein in his blood. She pointed out the dozens of packets dripping this and that into his body.

She said that a diagnosis of cancer had not been made, but the multiple problems pointed to possible cancer.

She asked Jack to confirm his decision to have the plugs pulled if matters came to that. He confirmed.

Then she engaged Jack in conversation by praising him for being an academic. He refused the praise by enumerating all the ghastly things that had gone wrong for him in that profession.

Then she inquired about his spiritual life (he's in a Catholic hospital), and Mark and I braced ourselves for his "plastic Jesus" riff, but no. Instead, he told her about how humans had raised themselves up by death, i.e., all the dead amoebas that evolution had caused. She offered the hospital's pastor who would come around if Jack wanted.

She left, and while we were waiting for the nurse to come turn Jack in bed to relieve his bedsores, he regaled us by singing this chorus from "There is a Tavern in the Town."

Fare thee well, for I must leave thee,

Do not let this parting grieve thee,

And remember that the best of friends

Must part, must part.

Adieu, adieu kind friends, yes, adieu

I can no longer stay with you, stay with you,

I`ll hang my harp on the weeping willow tree,

And may the world go well with thee.

—Marilyn June Coffey

Part III: Mourning Jack

Jack Loscutoff

April 7, 1931–September 9, 2015

Wednesday, September 9, 2015, 8:20 p.m.
JACK

My beloved Jack just died this evening.

NOTHING BUT THE FACTS

Jack Loscutoff
April 7, 1931–September 9, 2015

Born in San Francisco
Died in Omaha, Nebraska

JACK LOSCUTOFF

1931: I was born at an early age in San Francisco, California, of humble Russian peasant stock. If my grandparents had remained in the old country, I might be writing this in Russian instead of English. I prefer English because it's a much richer language than Russian.

Though I have other personae (Greek for "masks") as we all do, I especially like the creator mask. In me, it appears principally as wordsmith: poet, satirist, cartoonist, fool, teller of twelve-year-olds' bad jokes, minstrel, memoirist, essayist, comedian, playwright, short story writer, novelist, prophet, dreamer, teacher. But until my fifty-eighth birthday, I didn't create. Instead, I interpreted and evaluated the written words of others.

1967: San Francisco State College recognized my expertise as a literary critic by awarding me an MA in English and American literature. The most obvious employment for a person with that newly acquired skill was as a teacher of English composition, that is, essay writing at a community college. A semester of practice teaching at San Mateo Community College a few miles south of the big city convinced me it wasn't my cup of tea. The students (surprise, surprise) were no more prepared to write something interesting a month after graduating from high school than they were the month before.

Refusing to lower myself to teaching such dunderheads, I resolved to continue my own education and travel the road to a PhD. With that degree, I reasoned, I could work at a four-year college or university with serious, well-prepared

students. By then, however, my GI benefits had run out. I applied for and obtained a student loan. But even with the loan, I needed to earn additional money. For by then I had a wife and two small children.

I thought that problem was solved when I was accepted as a graduate teaching assistant at Washington University in St. Louis. The graduate teaching assistantship was an arrangement by which a student could work toward the degree half-time and teach the other half in exchange for a small salary and free tuition. In practice it amounted to teaching three-fourths time and studying one-quarter time. I left Washington U. after two years.

1969: I found a job at South Dakota State University teaching the same kinds of courses that I had sought to avoid at San Mateo Community College: English composition. The South Dakota students were no more prepared or serious than the California ones. They were certainly more culturally isolated. I got the axe after five years because the legislature ran out of money for teaching their young people how to write. Balancing the budget was more important.

1989: Fifteen years later on my fifty-eighth birthday, I realized I'd always been a bridesmaid but never a bride. And so, instead of being paralyzed by my awe of gods like Shakespeare, Dante, Melville, and Yeats, I made a decision. I would begin my climb up the Mount Olympus from which they looked down on me. Starting in 1989 with help from books on the subject and attendance at writing critique groups, I've been teaching myself creative writing. I haven't reached the top of the mountain, but sometimes I see the gods smiling in approval. That's reward enough.

JACK LOSCUTOFF
SAGE IN BLOOM
AUTHOR
POET

Performances:

"Semper Fidelis," a one-act play performed by Rough Magic Productions, Lincoln, Nebraska, 2006

"My Heart's in the Highlands," a one-act play, read on stage at the Great Plains Theatre Conference, Omaha, Nebraska, 2008

Thursday, September 10, 12:44 p.m.

Slept six hours last night, thanks to the teeny eeny weeny pill my doctor prescribed for just such occasions. It melts on my tongue, and I melt into the sheets.

Thursday, September 10, 8:21 p.m.

When I woke this morning after yesterday's Godawful loss, I felt as though I'd been struck on the back of my head with a two-by-four. It's better now, although my ears are ringing. But they always ring. I have tinnitus.

Thursday, September 10, 8:33 p.m.

FORGETFULNESS

Opened email this evening to find it swarming with messages and so was my Facebook. I know you didn't mean to make me cry, but cry I did to be surrounded by so much love and warmth. My gratitude feels boundless.

Thursday, September 10, 10:21 p.m.

I went for a walk today. When I got back, I found my house key still sticking in the lock. I'd left it there when returning home from having seen Jack for the last time. I think I left the key in the lock in case Jack changed his mind about leaving me.

Friday, September 11, 9:22 a.m.

In the middle of the night, I woke to watch Jack's body enter the crematorium furnace. I felt a scream rising. Then I remembered someone's advice: deep breaths. So I breathed deep, long slow yoga breaths. The image faded. I didn't have to weep wildly or call the Boys Town Hot Line. Since the occasion called for an eensy teeny pill, I took one, turned on my *Ocean Waves*, and went back to sleep.

Friday, September 11, 5:36 p.m.

Letter to Poet Lyn Lifshin

Sure, Lyn, it's hard, waking in the night to see Jack disappear into the crematorium furnace, but you know how poets love the dramatic. I didn't tell you how good it felt that night to pull off my sock and release my foot to air. Or how funny it was to watch my cat lead the way to her food bowl. Etc. A hundred pleasures per day, or more, to offset the occasional pain.

Nor did I mention my helpers. I connected with Zen Buddhism in 1959 and have participated in Hatha Yoga since the mid-1960s, using a mantra given to me then. All these resources remain with me to help me through the rough spots. I love my memory of lying in a yoga class in the grass outside a Hindu temple, the sun warming my face, the temple music in my ears, my breath slow and easy.

Besides these inner resources, I have more friends than I knew I had. So many people have written to me, my email inbox bulges. I haven't the stamina to answer each message, but I read each one and remember the writer. So much solace.

Plus music. Classical, jazz, the notes swirl around my days.

So Lyn, dear, in short, please take my wails with a pinch of salt.

Saturday, September 12, 7:27 a.m.

Applause

Please! Some applause!

I slept straight through for six and one-half hours without needing a tiny pill.

Saturday, September 12, 10:41 a.m.

First Drive

This morning, I drove my car for the first time since Jack entered Hospice House. Backed out. OK. Headed down the street when I noticed Jack sitting beside me in the passenger seat, his home away from home. He was all slouched down.

"Whatchu you doing here?" I asked.

He said what he used to say to me habitually, sometimes to my annoyance, "Drive safely." And we drove on.

Saturday, September 12, 9:56 p.m.

Here I am at OM, Omaha Healing Arts Center with David Loyd (center) and Lobsang Wangchuk, mourning Jack. David brought me to OM to watch the Tibetan Buddhist guys create a mandala from bits of colored sand. I bought a statue of the Green Tara to take home with me, for consolation.

Sunday, September 13, 8:39 a.m.
I Just Do

So it's 7 a.m. I'm lying in bed trying not to think about Jack so I can catch another hour or so of sleep, when there he is. Standing in the middle of my bedroom. In his clown posture, belting out, "I don't know why I love you like I do. I don't know why, I just do."

I reach out and touch his cheek. Stubble. Unshaven for the last week.

I wake at 8:22.

Sunday, September 13, 1:35 p.m.
Groceries

Didn't expect grocery shopping to be tough, but it was.

Walking by the motorized cart stand where Jack waited for me.

Selecting some paper towels with no bickering about price or brand.

Stopping by the display of candy that he couldn't resist.

#1 Trepidation

I dreaded visiting #235 at Crown Pointe, Jack's apartment. That's where I'd last seen Jack alive, before Bergan Mercy and the hospice.

That day he stood looking at his bed, a hospital bed, ample for one person, narrow for two. But possible. I knew that from running upstairs, when we lived together, and slipping in beside him when I needed comfort.

"Hmmm." He slid his hand under my clothes. "Wonder if we could both get in there."

"Sure!" I snuggled up against him.

"How?"

"Easy! Just take off our clothes and jump in."

He laughed and hugged me, he who could no longer put on or take off his socks.

So I dreaded going to his apartment. I dare not go alone. I just knew I'd crumple up and weep the moment I opened his door. So I asked Jack's son, Mark Loscutoff, to take me.

#2 The Poet

Jack owned more than four hundred books, but I wanted only one, Jack's favorite poetry book, *Rubáiyát of Omar Khayyám*, translated by Edward Fitzgerald in the nineteenth century.

Omar Khayyám, a Persian poet, a Sufi mystic, a mathematician, a philosopher, and an astronomer, lived from 1048 to 1131.

I encountered him in college, where I read lines like, "Your children are not your children," which enabled me to raise my son, Michael Henshaw. I wanted some of Omar Khayyám's poetry read at my wedding, but the pastor absolutely refused.

However, Omar Khayyám meant much more to Jack than to me. The Persian poet's "Be happy for this moment. This moment is your life" became Jack's credo. He often yanked the *Rubáiyát* off the shelf to read something to himself or to me. He even stuck pages of his notes in the book.

In fact, the Persian poet's book meant so much to Jack that I stole it when he left my house for Crown Pointe. I rationalized that I'd stolen it so it wouldn't get lost in the chaos of moving, but when Jack visited me, I made sure to hide the book.

Eventually I relented, fessed up, and returned the *Rubáiyát*. I knew right where in his apartment Jack put it, on his bookshelf next to the collected works of Marilyn June Coffey.

So all I wanted to do was go into Jack's apartment, grab that book, and leave.

#3 The Visit

So we three set out: me, Mark Loscutoff, and Paco Keopanya, my housemate and close friend. Across the lobby, with me in the lead, I took the stairs instead of the elevator to the second floor. I moved at a good clip, to much praise from the gentlemen behind me. I felt almost cheerful.

Mark unlocked the door. I walked past the bookcase and looked at the bed. Someone had made it. It didn't even look like Jack's bed, it was so tidy. I turned to his desk, took his fat collection of lyrics, a pocket-sized magnifying glass, and a few this and thats.

Then I walked to the window, past his expensive brand new chair-lift recliner that I'd bought for him. He had it for three or four days before he went to the hospital. What timing!

As I stood looking at Jack's exotic plants, I spotted the square end table I'd given to him when we still lived together, in an attempt to make him tidier. I'd lost that bet. The memory made me laugh, so I took the table home.

Then The Book. I plucked it out of the bookcase and turned to the boys, thinking I'd talk to them about it, but they were busy discussing Jack's computer. Did Paco want it? Should Mark sell it?

Later, at home, I brewed tea, sat, and opened the *Rubáiyát of Omar Khayyám*. Here's what I read:

The Moving Finger writes; and, having writ,

Moves on: nor all thy Piety nor Wit,

Shall lure it back to cancel half a Line,

Nor all thy Tears wash out a Word of it.

Wednesday, September 16, 1:10 p.m.
Jack's Houseplants

I found a splendid home for Jack's exotic houseplants.

Paco is delivering them to Deirdre Evans who, in turn, will give them to her friend Paula Cellar.

Here's what Deirdre wrote to me:

I would take some. Not for myself but for my friend Paula Cellar. She has multiple disabilities and uses a wheelchair now but one of her talents and love is taking care of houseplants. They thrive and flower for her.

I'm delighted, and I suspect Jack is even more delighted than I am. He loved those plants.

Friday, September 18, 11:05 p.m.
I'm So Chicken

How shall I mourn Jack? Some outward sign of my inward grief, I thought.

Wearing black? But when I looked at Internet images, they mirrored another era: long flowing skirts, veils over faces, no one in lanky black pants.

Then I saw that a bereaved person could make jewelry from the hair of her beloved, but I couldn't do that; Jack's hair had disappeared with Jack into the crematorium.

I almost didn't notice the third option: shave your head.

However, once the idea hit, it refused to leave. Visions of shaving my head whirred in my mind, some negative, some positive. I mentioned my thoughts to no one.

Finally I turned to my calendar, found the first possible date I could visit a beauty salon. Then I told myself, "Okay, Marilyn, on that date you either go get your hair shaved off or you shut up about it."

The morning of my free day, I went to my local Great Clips.

"Want a haircut?" the stylist asked.

I moved my hands all over my head. "Off. All off."

She nodded. That was a relief. For all I knew, Great Clips might refuse to shave my head, send me to a special barber for such a task.

"Will I need a shampoo?"

She looked quizzically at me.

"You know, to wash all the hair off."

"Nah." She wrote me in. "There's a forty-minute wait."

I waited.

Then, in the chair, I told Melissa what I wanted, and why, and watched my white locks fly to the floor. She ran a big clipper over my head, but I could still see a residue of hair. Then she picked up a small trimmer.

"Do you want your hair entirely off?" she asked. "I could leave

about this much" she pinched her fingers almost together, "with this trimmer."

I knew I should say, "Entirely off." I was, after all, shaving my head. Down to the skull. That's how it was done. The nerve, for even asking.

"Use the trimmer," I said, mortified. How could I be so spineless, so faint-hearted, so weak-kneed, so chicken-hearted.

Melissa trimmed away. "Oh, see how different you look. Your eyes! You can really see them. They're beautiful."

Her tip flew upward.

I looked at my face. I didn't look as ugly as I thought I would. Familiar, even. With my new beautiful eyes.

The stylist put down her trimmer and whipped off the black robe. "You'll be wearing a wig?"

A wig? That wouldn't be an outward sign of my inward grief, but I mollified her. "Hats!" I said. "I have lots of hats."

I ran my hands over the fuzz on my skull. I felt lightheaded. I felt happy. I even knew what Jack would say if he saw me like this. He'd say, as usual, "You're gorgeous." And I, as usual, wouldn't contradict him.

Here's my photo.

Or, as Greg Kosmicki would say, the photo of a "lovely old bald-headed poet woman!"

Sunday, September 20, 10:21 a.m.

Old Abe

Pulled into my driveway and what did I see? Jack, tall and skinny as Abraham Lincoln, scissoring over my garage roof.

"Jack!" I want to call, but I don't.

The Rail Splitter is in a rush, slicing across my big backyard and chopping through the trees.

Four Nurses

Woke in the middle of the night. Saw four identical thick-waisted, middle-aged, white-garbed nurses sitting side by side on a long, narrow wooden bench.

"Whatcha doing?" I call.

"Taking care of Jack," they chorus.

The Walk

Crisp, clear autumn day. I'm stepping right along on my forty-minute daily exercise walk, repeating my Sanskrit mantra, *om mani padme hum*. My mantra is a blessing; it replaces my thoughts and reminds me to be one with the world.

About halfway up the hill, I sense Jack beside me. I think, "Oh, this will never work. Jack can't keep up with me on his useless legs."

"Get this." Jack points to his feet. I look down. He's standing on a skateboard. "Let's go!"

And off he zooms, showoff as usual, twirling and stomping in the intersection.

He returns and slips his hand inside my pants, halfway to my crack, a favorite position. And off we go: *om mani padme hum, om mani padme hum, om mani padme hum.*

ༀ་མ་ཎི་པ་དྨེ་ཧཱུྂ

Tuesday, September 22, 3:11 p.m.

JACK'S GARDEN

Sometime last spring, Jack brought home a half-dozen plants and showed me the bedraggled little things. *Portulaca grandiflora*, he said. They looked like moss roses to me. They were so ugly, I wondered why he'd bought them.

He scooped up one from its container. "From Brazil. Or maybe Argentina."

I had to laugh. Jack never bought sensible American plants. He preferred tropical plants like crotons, bromeliads, or elephant ears. Many of his exotics died on him, so I expected these floppy little plants would too.

Jack touched my arm and spoke softly. "Where do you want me to put them?"

I sighed. "How about your office? The living room's jam packed."

"No, outdoors." He grinned at my surprised look.

"Outdoors?" I shrugged. "Oh, anywhere you want except my rose garden." My rose garden. I'd managed not to kill my eighteen inherited roses for a decade. Irish luck. My former husband called me The Black Thumb, and he was right. The only plants I can grow are things like aloe vera. Jade. Rickrack. They're all succulents. Indifferent to this distracted gardener.

I followed Jack out, watched him select a dirt rectangle near the front porch. An unlikely spot. Nothing ever grew there but weeds.

"That'll be too dry for them, Jack." I thrust my chest forward. "That overhang blocks the rain." "It should be okay," he mumbled, dirt flying as he dug holes. "Nice and sunny."

I went inside.

Jack became a mad man. He could barely kneel, but every day I'd see him kneeling beside those portulacas, fussing, weeding, doing the things he did to plants, things I had no patience for. When I stood watching him, he reached over to pat my leg. "I just want to make sure they root, honey."

Then just before Jack moved to Crown Pointe, he took my hand and led me to the front porch. We stood and looked down on his portulacas, sprawling in the sun. A few bloomed. "Will you take care of them for me?" He squeezed me.

Bummer. Just one more bloody chore! I wanted to say, "Take care of your own damn portulacas. I don't even know how." But I said, "Sure."

Once or twice over the summer, Jack asked me how the portulacas were doing. "Have the roots set?"

And I, who never looked at them, replied, "They're fine, Jack, just fine."

Once I even stepped out on the porch and took a gander to see if I were lying. The funny little plants with their limp stems had burst into bloom: dozens of flowers in all colors, red, yellow, orange, pink, purple, and white. Astonishing!

When I returned for the last time from Hospice House to my home, I glanced at Jack's portulaca garden, suddenly remembering my promise to take care of it.

Weeds choked his blooms: two crabgrass plants, their tall skinny spikes twirling in the breeze, a huge many-layered dandelion rosette that would take some uprooting to kill, and pig weed. I think that's what it's called, dozens of those plants, their long lazy fingers flat against the ground, surrounding and penetrating Jack's portulacas.

I wasted no time. For several days I carefully pulled weeds, not wanting to accidentally rip out the flowers. When the garden was empty of everything but blooms, I mulched the empty spaces.

And just for the heck of it, I looked up *Portulaca grandiflora*. Hmph! Moss rose, just as I thought.

To my surprise, moss roses are something even a black thumb like me could grow: they're succulents.

ACKNOWLEDGMENTS

I wish to thank those readers of my blog, a *JoLt of CoFFeY*, who first suggested I collect my posts about Jack into book form. They planted the seed.

In particular, I'm grateful to first readers Barbara "Bee" Lanning, and Sandra "Sandy" Wendel for their enthusiasm, and Michael "Mike" Skau for his reading of my poems.

Thanks also to Dr. Dennis McNeilly, who suggested I find illustrations for my book.

Among those who helped me fashion this book are Lisa Pelto, CEO, Rachel Moore, designer, Sandra Wendel, editor, and all of Concierge Marketing in Omaha. Plus Paula Wallace, the illustrator. A slew of appreciation.

And of course, *JackJack & JuneBug* could never have been written without Jack Loscutoff, his poems and his love.

www.ingramcontent.com/pod-product-compliance
Lightning Source LLC
Chambersburg PA
CBHW041531090426
42738CB00036B/120